Love Lines

Mr. Owl

PARAS PANDYA

DEDICATION

I dedicate all these poems to those beautiful people

who believe in love and love someone.

ACKNOWLEDGMENT

Dear Readers,

What is LOVE LINES ? Well, simply put, love lines are feelings, emotions, respect, care, life, intimate lines and verses of poetry or prose full of love and passion, written from the heart. This isn't just a book—it's a piece of me, raw and unfiltered. it's Emotions. These poems don't follow rules. No fancy structure, no rhymes, just fast and strong feelings with lots of emotions laid bare.

Take your time here. Read slowly. Let go of expectations. Don't rush to find meaning in every line. These words need to breathe. Stay with the verses that move you, come back to the ones that don't, and carry the ones that heal you.

They are full of desires and fantasies, soft, sensual whispers and promises, evoking imagery of love longed for and love lost.

Penned by noted author, poet, and aspiring writer Paras Pandya were written with a flair

PROLOGUE

I wrote the poem when I was missing her, But when I tried to understand her feelings and how delicate our love was for each other. Tears welled up in my eyes. Even today, whenever I remember her, I cry silently.

I must let you go because I love you and wish you all the best, no matter wherever you are, without telling, how much I love you and without you, how I will be shattered.

Finally, I wiped my tears and came on the roof. Under the sunlight. I became one of the biggest losers, who lost everything in love and life. But I was satisfied because, after going away from her to me, at least she would be always happy.

Whatever happened, I am still grateful to her because she was the one with whom I fell in love. She is not with me and she will never turn up I know but I still love her and will continue to love her. She has gone, not her love......It's always with me.

My heart beats only for you..

You are my dream,
My wish come true..

Like chai in rain, you bring me peace,
In your love, my heart finds ease.

Love is sweet, love is kind,
You are always on my mind.

Your touch is soft, like petals fair,
My heart is light when you are near.

In your hug,

I find my home,
Never again will I feel alone.

You and me,

Like rangoli bright,
Filling life with love and light.

Your love is warm,

Like morning chai,
One sip of you, and I fly high.

My heart beats fast when you are near,
Your love is music to my ear.
Like monsoon breeze, you touch my soul,
With you, my heart is always whole.
Holding hands, we walk so free,
You and I, it's destiny.
Your voice is sweet, like temple bells,
In your love, my heart swells.
Stars may fade and rivers dry,
But my love will never die.

You and me,
Like rose and red,
Love so deep,
Nothing to dread.

In your love,

I lose my way,
But in your arms,

I wish to stay.

that will seductively entice all lovers of intimate, romantic poetry and prose to journey on a voyage filled with candlelit nights, candid conversation and sensuality that will romantically caress one's heart and mind, while at the same time touching the soul of the most tender of lovers. This isn't one story—it's a collection of moments and emotions. it's a love lines. Maybe you'll see yourself in them. Maybe they'll remind you of something lost, or something you're still holding on to.

This book, it's more than poetry—it's a bridge between us. This is my heart on the page, and as you read, it becomes yours too.

With all this love,

Mr. Owl

Your love is sweet, like sugar and tea,
You are the only one for me.
My heart is yours, please take it all,
Without you, my world feels small.

Your love is like the Ganga's flow,

Forever pure, forever so.

Like peacock dancing in the rain,

Your love takes away my pain.

You are the moon, I am the tide,

Always with you, side by side.

My love for you will never bend,
From start of time to the very end.

You and I,
like birds so free,
Together forever,
we are meant to be.

With you,
My love,
Life is bright,

Every
Moment
Feels so right.

Your touch is soft,
Your love so deep,
In your arms,
I wish to sleep.

My heart is yours,
Please take the key,
Together forever,
Just you and me.

You are my prayer,
My temple light,

My sun in day,
My moon at night.

With you,
My heart feels so right.

My heart beats fast when you are near,
Your love is music to my ear.
Holding you close, I have no fear.

No need for words, our eyes do say,
"I love you now and every day."
With you, my love, I wish to stay.

Unseen Love

I look at you, but you don't see,
A love so deep, it sets me free.
Every smile you give, I save,
Yet in your heart, I have no place.
Still, I love you, quiet and true,
Even if you never knew.

A Silent Prayer

I whisper your name in the evening breeze,
Hoping the wind carries it with ease.
My heart beats only for you,
Yet you never hear its tune.
Even in pain, my love stays pure,
A silent prayer that longs for you.

Waiting for You

Like monsoon clouds waiting to pour,
I stand at your door, hoping for more.
Your laughter fills my lonely sky,
Yet you walk past, not knowing why
I hide my love, I smile and say,
"May you find happiness every day."

A Love Untold

Every time our eyes do meet,
My heart skips a thousand beats.
But you look away, unaware,
Of the love that lingers there.
I wish I had the words to say,
That I love you in every way.

Like the Moon

I am the moon, you are the sun,
Close yet distant, never one.
I shine for you, night and day,
But you chase the light away.
Still, I wait, in silent pain,
Hoping you will look again.

Just a Friend

You tell me stories of love so true,
Of someone else, not me and you.
I smile and laugh, hiding the pain,
Wishing you'd love me the same.
But as a friend, I stay right here,
Loving you from far, yet near.

The Pain of Loving You

If love is joy, why do I weep?
Why does my heart ache so deep?
You walk by, lost in your world,
While I remain, a love unfurled.
Yet, even if you never see,
I will love you endlessly.

A Wish Upon a Star

Each night, I wish upon a star,
That you would love me from afar.
But stars don't change what's meant to be,
And you are not meant for me.
Still, I hope, still, I dream,
Though love remains a silent scream.

A Love That Fades in Shadows

I walk beside you, step by step,
Hiding feelings my heart has kept.
You turn to others, smile so bright,
But never see my silent fight.
One day, my love may fade away,
But until then, here I stay.

A Letter Never Sent

I write my love in words so deep,
But keep them locked where secrets sleep.
If only you could read my heart,
You'd know we were never apart.
But letters burn and words decay,
Yet my love will never sway.

Your Happiness First

If love means letting go,
Then I will watch the river flow.
You love another, I can see,
Yet still, you mean the world to me.
If you're happy, that's enough,
Even if my heart stays rough.

Chasing Shadows

I follow your footsteps, lost in the race,
But you never turn to see my face.
You chase a love that's far from view,
And I chase a dream—only you.
One-sided love is cruel and cold,
Yet my heart refuses to fold.

A Name I Whisper

Your name is a song my lips still hum,
Even though you never come.
Every street reminds me of you,
Yet to you, I'm just someone you knew.
Still, I whisper, still, I dream,
Loving you in ways unseen.

If You Knew

If you knew the way I feel,
Would your heart begin to heal?
Or would you turn, walk away,
Leaving me to fade away?
I love you, but I stay apart,
Holding back my fragile heart.

Not Meant to Be

I love you like the waves love shore,
But reach you, I can nevermore.
You love another, I see it clear,
Yet still, my heart keeps you near.
Some loves are never meant to be,
But still, they live eternally.

A Rose Without a Name

I place a rose where you will pass,
Hoping you'll notice, but you walk fast.
You never see, you never know,
The love that silently grows.
Like petals lost in morning dew,
My heart still aches, only for you.

The Sound of Your Laughter

Your laughter is my favorite song,
Though it never plays for me for long.
You laugh with them, you smile so free,
While my love stays a mystery.
Still, I cherish every sound,
Even if I stay background.

Your Eyes, My World

When you look at me, my heart soars high,
But you look away, and I sigh.
Your eyes are stars, bright and true,
Yet they never shine for me, only you.
Still, in their glow, I lose my way,
Loving you more every day.

The Words I Can't Say

A thousand words stay in my chest,
Yet I smile and hide the rest.
You see a friend, you see my cheer,
But never notice my hidden tear.
One-sided love is silent pain,
A story written in unseen rain.

Still, I Love You

No promises, no words are said,
Yet in my heart, you live instead.
Even if you love another face,
Even if I have no place,
Still, my love will never fade,
Like sunshine lost in evening shade.

Forever Waiting

I loved you then, I love you now,
Through every season, every vow.
Years have passed, but still, I stand,
A love so strong, yet never planned.
You smile at me, but not the same,
For you, it's friendship, not love's flame.
Yet, even if you never see,
My heart still beats for you and me.

A Love That Never Fades

I have loved you since the first hello,
Through days of sunshine, nights of woe.
I hide my love, I wear a smile,
But my heart breaks all the while.
You hold another close and near,
Yet still, I wish you'd see me here.
No matter how the time may flow,
My love for you will only grow.

A Silent Devotion

Years have passed, yet I remain,
Loving you through joy and pain.
You look at me, yet never see,
The love that lives so silently.
I watch you chase your dreams so high,
And wish that I could be your sky.
But you will never turn my way,
Still, I love you—come what may.

A Love That Time Can't Change

They say that time can heal all pain,
Yet my love for you still remains.
Each moment spent, each word you said,
Still echoes softly in my head.
You move ahead, while I stand still,
Loving you against my will.
Yet even if my heart must break,
This love of mine, none can take.

My Heart Belongs to You

No matter how the years may fly,
My love for you will never die.
I see you smile, I hear you speak,
Yet you don't know the love I keep.
I stand so near, yet feel so far,
Loving you from where you are.
You'll never know, you'll never see,
But my heart is yours eternally.

You in Shadows

You have lived inside my heart,
Yet we remain so far apart.
You laugh, you shine, you dance so free,
Unaware of what you mean to me.
Years may come, and years may go,
But my love will only grow.
Even if I fade away,
My love for you will always stay.

A Love Never Spoken

If only you could read my eyes,
You'd see the love I cannot hide.
But words are weak, and fate is cruel,
I stand in love, yet play the fool.
You love another, this I know,
Yet still, my heart won't let you go.
A lifetime spent, yet you're unaware,
Of the love that lingers in the air.

Unanswered Love

I have loved you through every tide,
Through every tear I've learned to hide.
You call me friend, and nothing more,
Yet my heart stays where it was before.
I wait for words you'll never say,
Still, I love you every day.
Even if my love is lost,
I'll love you, no matter the cost.

A Love That Won't Die

Through changing times, through endless pain,
My love for you will stay the same.
You live your life, you chase your dreams,
While I stay lost in silent screams.
Even if the world should end,
I'll still love you, my dearest friend.
A love so pure, a love so true,
Even time can't take me from you.

Loving You from Afar

Like the moon that loves the sea,
You are too far away from me.
Yet still, I shine, I stay, I glow,
Loving you though you don't know.
You walk past me, lost in thought,
While I hold on to dreams I've fought.
Even if my heart must break,
Loving you was no mistake.

A Heart That Stays Behind

The world moves fast, the seasons change,
But my love for you stays the same.
You have found your place to be,
Yet I still dream of you and me.
I see you happy, I see you bright,
Yet in my heart, there is no light.
Still, I stay, still, I wait,
Loving you is my fate.

If Only You Knew

If only you could see my heart,
You'd know we were never apart.
Though distance grows, though time moves on,
My love for you is never gone.
You live your life without a clue,
That someone waits and loves you true.
Even if you never see,
I will love you endlessly.

A Love Without End

I have loved you for so long,
Yet to you, I don't belong.
You see the world with joyful eyes,
Unaware of my silent cries.
I hold my heart, I walk alone,
A love unspoken, still unknown.
No matter where life takes you now,
My love will stay—this is my vow.

The Love You Never Saw

I have walked beside you, step by step,
Through love unspoken, feelings kept.
You held another, laughed so free,
While I stood there, lost in me.
You never saw, you never knew,
That all my love was meant for you.
Yet even now, I will not leave,
For loving you is what I believe.

Fear of the Fall

I fear the fall, the way love can break,
A heart so fragile, too much at stake.
You smile at me, and I look away,
Fearing the feelings I can't betray.
What if love comes and leaves me cold?
Can I face the pain, can I be bold?

A Heart Unwilling

My heart beats fast, but I hesitate,
Scared of love and the pain it can create.
I've seen hearts torn, pieces in the wind,
And I wonder if I'll face that end.
Yet, you stand near, and I want to fall,
But fear holds me back, a silent wall.

The Fear of Losing Myself

What if I lose myself in you?
What if my love makes me forget what's true?
I fear the change, the way love can steal,
The parts of me I’ve learned to feel.
But here you are, so close, so near,
And still, I fight this overwhelming fear.

The Fear of Heartbreak

My heart is heavy, yet I want to soar,
But love is a risk, a dangerous door.
What if you leave, what if you go?
And I'm left alone, with nothing to show.
I want to trust, I want to believe,
But I fear the hurt that love can weave.

Holding Back

I see you, I feel the spark,
But love's a fire that can leave a mark.
What if I fall and lose my way?
What if tomorrow, you walk away?
I stand on the edge, but I can't leap,
Afraid that my heart's too fragile to keep.

Unspoken Love

I love you in silence, too scared to say,
For love, sometimes, just fades away.
The fear of opening my heart so wide,
Is too much to bear, so I hide.
But here I stand, trembling inside,
Wanting to love, but too scared to try.

Running from Love

I see you and feel my heart race,
But I turn away, not ready to face,
The feelings I fear will take me apart,
The possibility of breaking my heart.
I run, I hide, though love calls me near,
Scared that it's not worth the fear.

The Walls I Build

I build walls around my heart,
Hoping love will stay apart.
I want to feel, but I am scared,
Of being vulnerable and unprepared.
So, I keep my distance, close yet far,
Fearing the pain, loving from a scar.

Afraid to Fall

Love is a leap, a risk I can’t take,
What if it breaks me, what if I break?
I’ve seen hearts crushed, I’ve seen them fall,
And I wonder if I can face it all.
But still, you call, you make me want to fly,
Yet I fear love’s answer is goodbye.

A Hesitant Heart

My heart is a traveler, afraid of the road,
Scared of the pain that love might unload.
What if I trust and it turns to dust?
What if love leaves me in the rust?
So, I stay back, not letting you near,
Fearing the hurt, the doubt, the fear.

Shattered Pieces

My heart is broken, scattered in dust,
A soul once whole, now lost in rust.
I loved too deeply, trusted too much,
Now, every memory feels like a touch.
Each moment spent feels like a scar,
And I wonder if I'll ever heal, near or far.

The Silent Scream

I scream inside, but no one hears,
A soul shattered by endless fears.
The love I gave, now torn apart,
Leaving nothing but a broken heart.
I wish for peace, I wish for calm,
But all I feel is endless alarm.

Crushed by Love

My heart was full, now it's just a shell,
A love once perfect, now gone to hell.
The pain of loss, it cuts so deep,
A wound that never lets me sleep.
I gave it all, but you took it away,
Leaving me in darkness, unable to stay.

Falling Apart

Like glass that shatters on the floor,
My soul breaks, unable to restore.
Each shard of hope, each broken dream,
Reminds me of how cruel love can seem.
You walked away, and I was left,
A shell of myself, broken, bereft.

A Love Unraveled

Once tightly woven, my heart was whole,
Now it lies scattered, a broken soul.
The love I gave, so pure, so true,
Now feels like ashes, fading through.
I trusted you, but now I see,
That love has shattered the parts of me.

The Empty Echo

I hear your voice, but it's just a ghost,
A memory of a love I miss the most.
Every echo of your name cuts through,
A soul shattered by the loss of you.
I reach out, but you're not there,
Leaving me with nothing, only despair.

Lost in the Void

My soul once bright, now lost in gray,
A love that was real, now fades away.
I thought we'd last, thought we would grow,
But now I’m left with endless woe.
In the silence, I scream for you,
But it’s too late, you’ve left me too.

The Weight of Goodbye

Goodbyes are heavy, but yours was worse,
A soul-shattering pain, a heart's curse.
The love we had, the trust we shared,
Now gone, leaving me unprepared.
You walked away without a sound,
Leaving me lost, nowhere to be found.

Fading Hope

I held on tight, never letting go,
But now I'm fading, sinking slow.
The love I gave, the dreams I built,
Now feel like ashes, covered in guilt.
I gave my soul, but you didn't stay,
Now I'm left in pieces, lost and gray.

The Unspoken Pain

I never said it, but you knew it well,
That my heart was yours, under your spell.
Yet you left, without a word,
A silence louder than what I heard.
Now my soul is torn apart,
A love unspoken, breaking my heart.

All This Love

All this love, too deep to speak,
A feeling so strong, yet so weak.
It lifts me high, then lets me fall,
A fire that burns, but feels so small.
I give my heart, I give my soul,
But love, it takes, it never makes me whole.

The Weight of Love

All this love, it weighs me down,
A golden crown, a painted frown.
It pulls me close, then sets me free,
A dance of pain, a mystery.
I wanted joy, but found the ache,
Yet still, I love, for love's own sake.

Love's Silent Call

All this love, it calls so loud,
A whisper soft, yet not allowed.
It haunts my dreams, it fills my mind,
A feeling I can't leave behind.
It's every breath, it's every tear,
A love that's endless, yet unclear.

All This Heartache

All this love, it leaves me cold,
A story written, yet untold.
It fills my heart, then breaks it too,
A shattered dream, a sky once blue.
But even through the hurt I face,
I hold on tight, in love's embrace.

A Love That Holds

All this love, a gentle chain,
It holds me close, it numbs the pain.
It builds me up, then lets me fall,
It's everything, yet nothing at all.
I long for peace, I crave for rest,
But love, it holds me, keeps me blessed.

The Longing

All this love, it pulls me near,
A touch so soft, yet filled with fear.
I reach for you, but you slip away,
Like morning mist that fades to gray.
I wait in silence, I hope, I sigh,
For all this love, I can't deny.

A Heart's Desire

All this love, a heart's desire,
A flame that burns, a never-ending fire.
I wish to touch, to feel, to know,
But love's path is crooked, slow.
It gives me joy, it gives me pain,
But still, I love, again and again.

The Giving

All this love, a sacrifice,
A gift of trust, a roll of dice.
I give my all, I give my best,
Yet in your heart, I find no rest.
Love's not fair, love's not kind,
But still, I love, and still, I find.

The Boundless Love

All this love, it has no end,
A feeling shared with every friend.
It's in the laugh, it's in the tears,
A love that's known throughout the years.
It lifts, it falls, it rises high,
All this love will never die.

The Sweetest Pain

All this love, it's bittersweet,
A constant pull, a steady beat.
It's joy, it's sorrow, it's all of me,
A pain I long to set free.
But even in the hurt I feel,
All this love, it's all so real.

You're My Hope

In the darkest night, you are my light,
When the world seems wrong, you make it right.
You're my hope, my guiding star,
No matter how near, no matter how far.
In your love, I find my way,
You're my hope, come what may.

The Heart That Knows

You're my hope when I lose my way,
A steady hand when skies are gray.
In every storm, you are my calm,
A soothing touch, a healing balm.
With you beside me, I stand tall,
You're my hope, my heart's call.

Through Every Storm

When the storm is fierce and the winds blow strong,
You're my hope, where I belong.
Through every tear, through every fight,
You are my strength, my heart's delight.
In your love, I find my ground,
You're my hope, my soul unbound.

My Silent Prayer

You're my hope, my silent prayer,
In every breath, you're always there.
When life gets tough, and dreams fade
away,
You lift me up, you guide my way.
With every step, your love I feel,
You're my hope, my heart's seal.

You Are My Dawn

You're my hope, the light of dawn,
The reason I keep holding on.
In your eyes, I see my dreams,
You're my hope, or so it seems.
In every whisper, every glance,
You're my hope, my soul's dance.

The Quiet Heart

There is love in silence, soft and slow,
A whisper that only my heart can know.
It's in the way I watch you from afar,
Admiring the beauty of who you are.
In every glance, in every smile,
I hold my breath for just a while.

You walk through life, unaware of me,
Your voice a melody, so wild and free.
But I stay quiet, afraid to speak,
For fear of breaking the love I seek.
Silent love, like a shadow's embrace,
A hidden joy, a quiet grace.

I watch you laugh, and I feel your pain,
Yet I cannot speak, I cannot explain.
My heart beats faster, my hands grow cold,
But I bury it deep, never to unfold.
This love, it stays locked, never free,
A secret I carry quietly.

Sometimes I wonder, do you feel me near?
Do you sense the love I hold, my dear?
But I keep my silence, I wear my mask,
Hoping someday you'll ask.
For now, I stay in shadows deep,
Loving you silently, my heart to keep.

A Love Unspoken

There are no words to tell you, no sound to make,
Just a quiet heart that quietly breaks.
I watch you from the edge of your life,
Wishing for a place where I could be your light.
But my love is silent, it never speaks,
It's a soft whisper, the one that seeks.

In every moment, I wish to be bold,
To tell you what my heart has longed to hold.
But fear grips me, and doubt takes control,
As I watch you walk, unaware of my soul.
My love for you is patient, it waits,
Staring at the stars, counting the fates.

I love you in silence, not by choice,
But because love doesn't always have a voice.
It hides in corners, in quiet places,
In the way my heart races.
Yet I never speak, I never show,
The silent love I'll never let go.

There are no letters, no words to say,
Only a heart that wishes you'd stay.
You may never know, you may never see,
How deeply I feel,

how much you mean to me.
But this love, it stays in the silent night,
A love unspoken, but burning bright.

The Unseen Love

I love you in silence, my heart a quiet song,
A melody no one can hear, but it plays all along.
You walk by, and I silently stand,
Wishing for the courage to reach out my hand.
But I stay still, lost in my fear,
Afraid that my love would disappear.

I see you smile, I see you laugh,
And it fills me with joy, yet a sadness in half.
For I know you don't feel the way I do,
But my love for you remains true.
Unseen, unnoticed, but always near,
A silent love I hold so dear.

There's no spoken word, no written letter,
No grand declaration, nothing better.
Just the quiet moments I cherish alone,
Watching you from a distance, yet never shown.
The love I feel, you'll never see,
But it's in every thought, every memory.

I want to tell you, I want to be known,
But in silence, I have grown.
I've learned to live with this quiet ache,
Hoping someday, you'll see the love I make.

Until that day, I remain unseen,
Loving you quietly, where you've never
been.

The Empty Silence

You were once the rhythm of my heart,
But now, I stand here, torn apart.
The days we shared feel far away,
Fading in the light of a brand new day.
I search for you, but you're not there,
Only emptiness fills the air.

I gave you everything, all my love,
Yet you chose to walk away, far above.
Your absence cuts, it hurts so deep,
A secret I keep, a wound I'll weep.
I thought forever was what we'd find,
But now I'm lost, with you behind.

You were my world, my hope, my dream,
But now, you're just a silent stream.
I try to move on, but your face stays,
Haunting my nights, clouding my days.
All that's left are memories fading,
Love lost, but never fully fading.

The Pieces of Us

I held you close, I thought we'd stay,
But now you're gone, and I feel betrayed.
The promises we made, now broken and
worn,
Leaving my heart, bruised and torn.
Once we were everything, two hearts as one,
Now I'm left with only what's undone.

I loved you with a strength so pure,
But your silence made my love unsure.
You slipped away with no goodbye,
Leaving me here, wondering why.
In the stillness, I hear no sound,
Just an aching heart, scattered on the
ground.

I search for the love that we once knew,
But now it's just me, missing you.
I remember the warmth, the touch of your
hand,
Now all that's left is shifting sand.
Love lost leaves a hole in the soul,
No matter how hard I try to make it whole.

Fading Dreams

I thought love was forever, a bond so tight,
But now it's just shadows, fading from
sight.
The laughter we shared, now lost in time,
A song unsung, a forgotten rhyme.
I gave you my trust, my heart, my all,
But now you've walked away, leaving me to
fall.

You were the dream I never thought would
end,
But love's cruel game has forced us to bend.
I stand here alone, holding on to the past,
Wondering why love couldn't last.
My heart still aches, even though you're
gone,
A love so strong, now feels withdrawn.

I keep the memories tucked inside,
But love lost is like a bitter tide.
I loved you deeply, with all my soul,
But now, I'm left to fill the hole.
Perhaps someday, I'll learn to breathe,
But for now, love's loss is all I grieve.

In Your Arms

Your touch is soft like a summer breeze,
Gentle on my skin, bringing me to my
knees.
I dream of your lips, a tender kiss,
A promise of love wrapped in bliss.
Your hands on my body, tracing each line,
In the still of the night, you are mine.

I feel the warmth of your breath on my neck,
A soft murmur, a secret we both keep in
check.
Every whisper, every sigh, so sweet,
In your arms, my heart skips a beat.
Promises linger, unspoken, but real,
I crave the love, the warmth you steal.

The Language of Desire

I want to lose myself in your touch,
Feel your hands, soft yet so much.
The way you pull me close, so tight,
I close my eyes and feel the night.
Your lips, so tender, I long to taste,
A slow kiss, like a sweet embrace.

Every caress is a story told,
A fantasy of love, both soft and bold.
The rhythm of our hearts, beating in time,
Our souls entwined in a dance sublime.
Promises whispered, not a word to say,
But in your touch, you lead the way.

Under the Moonlight

In the quiet night, under the moon's glow,
I imagine the way your fingers flow.
Tracing my skin with the softest grace,
Every touch ignites a flame in this place.
Your body close, your warmth I crave,
In your arms, I'm no longer brave.

I dream of the taste of your lips so sweet,
Of tangled sheets and hearts that meet.
A promise lingers in the cool night air,
To love you gently, to always care.
Soft whispers in the dark, dreams untold,
A love that's tender, a love so bold.

The Softness of You

In the quiet of the night, we find our space,
Where words are few, but hearts race.
Your touch, a whisper on my skin,
Inviting me to places we've never been.
The warmth of your hands, so gentle and
kind,
They trace my soul, they ease my mind.

You pull me close, and I breathe you in,
The scent of your skin, where love begins.
Your lips find mine, soft and slow,
A promise unspoken in the afterglow.
We move together in a rhythm divine,
In perfect sync, your heart in mine.

Every kiss ignites a flame so sweet,
A desire I crave, a love complete.
The world outside fades to nothing at all,
As I surrender to you, body and soul.
In every caress, in every sigh,
I lose myself in the depths of your eyes.

Your voice, so tender, calls my name,
In every whisper, we play love's game.
Your hands move gently, tracing every part,
Leaving imprints on both body and heart.
In the silence between our breaths, I know,
This is the love that will always grow.

We are two bodies, but one heart,
In this moment, we are never apart.
Each touch, each kiss, each fleeting sigh,
We find ourselves, you and I.
In the dance of our souls, we are entwined,
In intimate love, so pure, so kind.

The Language of Love

There are no words for what we feel,
In the space between us, love is real.
Your fingers brush my cheek, so light,
Sending shivers down my spine tonight.
No need for speech, no need for sound,
In your arms, I've found my ground.

Your lips trace paths along my skin,
And with each kiss, I feel you within.
The world outside is far away,
In your embrace, I choose to stay.
The rhythm of our hearts speaks loud,
In the silence, love is found.

I crave the taste of your every breath,
In the warmth of your touch, I forget death.
The closeness we share is beyond compare,
As you pull me closer, with tender care.
Our bodies collide in soft embrace,
Moving together in a sacred space.

Your hands explore, they gently roam,
In your touch, I find my home.
The softness of you, the strength you bring,
In our love, I feel everything.
We fall deeper with every move,
In this intimacy, we find our groove.

The moon above, the stars so bright,
But it's in your arms I find my light.
A thousand dreams dance in your eyes,
As we lose ourselves under these skies.
No words are needed to make it clear,
In the quiet love, you're always near.

In the depth of our love, we intertwine,
The softest of touches, the truest sign.
Here in this moment, our hearts are one,
And in the silence, love's journey's begun.
In the rhythm of us, there's no need to
speak,
For in our intimacy, we are complete.

A Dance of Desire

In the quiet of the night, where shadows fade,
I feel your presence, my heart starts to cascade.
Every touch of your fingers, soft on my skin,
A spark that ignites, where love begins.
You pull me close, your breath on my neck,
Every kiss is a promise, every touch a check.

In your arms, the world disappears,
Your love, your warmth, calms all my fears.
Your lips on mine, so gentle, so sweet,
I feel my soul lift, with every heartbeat.
You explore my body, each curve, each part,
As if you're painting a map of my heart.

Our bodies align, in rhythm so deep,
We move as one, the world fades to sleep.
Your hands trace my curves, your lips on my skin,
Every whisper, every sigh, pulls me in.
Your touch, so tender, your gaze, so sure,
In this moment, our love is pure.

The passion that rises, the heat in the air,
As we lose ourselves in each other's care.
The rhythm of love, of desire unbound,
We find our voices in silence profound.

In this dance, we are tangled, entwined,
A love so deep, it's one of a kind.

You hold me close, as our hearts race fast,
In your embrace, I feel at last.
The world may change, but this will stay,
Our love, our passion, in every way.
For in this dance of desire, we are one,
And nothing can break what we’ve begun.

The Heat Between Us

There's a fire that burns when you're near,
A heat that rises, a love sincere.
In every touch, in every glance,
I fall deeper into this trance.
You move so close, your breath so warm,
Every caress, a new love born.

Your hands on my skin, so soft, so sure,
A hunger, a need, so deep and pure.
You kiss me slow, then harder still,
I give myself to you, against my will.
Every inch of me, you claim as yours,
And in your love, I'm lost, I'm yours.

The passion that flows, like a river so wild,
It takes me in, it makes me a child.
Your body moves, your hands explore,
Every touch, I crave for more.
Our souls collide, our hearts entwine,
In your love, I find divine.

The heat between us, the fire we ignite,
A love that burns, through the deepest night.
In the quiet, our bodies speak,
Whispering love, both strong and weak.
Every kiss, every sigh, so deep,
In your love, my soul I keep.

We move together, a perfect rhyme,
As we lose ourselves in space and time.
In this moment, we are free,
Bound by love, just you and me.
Every touch, every caress, every kiss,
I feel the world in our love's bliss.

In the Quiet of You

The quiet of your love speaks so loud,
In every touch, a promise, unbowed.
Your hands, they find me in the dark,
And with every touch, you leave your mark.
The softness of your lips on mine,
A kiss so deep, a love divine.

We meet in silence, a thousand words
unsaid,
But in the quiet of your touch, my heart is
led.
Your fingers trace the path of my soul,
And with each caress, I lose control.
The depth of your love, the fire in your eyes,
It makes me fall, makes me rise.

In the quiet of you, I feel so whole,
A love so deep, it fills my soul.
Every kiss is a promise, every breath a vow,
In your arms, I'm lost, here and now.
Your love moves through me, soft yet bold,
A story written in touch, untold.

We explore the depths, the passions
unknown,
In your embrace, I'm never alone.
Your body on mine, your heart in sync,
Together we drift, together we sink.

In the heat of the moment, we are one,
A love like no other, never to be undone.

Your love is gentle, yet fierce and wild,
In every touch, I feel like a child.
Your hands on my skin, your lips on my
soul,
In this love, I lose all control.
In the quiet of you, in the silence we share,
I find a love beyond compare.

The Soft Touch

Your touch is like a gentle breeze,
It calms my heart, it puts me at ease.
In your arms, I find my home,
Where love speaks softly, and I'm not alone.
Each kiss is a promise, a vow so true,
In every moment, I feel you.

A Silent Connection

In the silence, we speak without words,
In your eyes, my soul is heard.
Every kiss, every touch, so kind,
Brings us closer, heart and mind.
You hold me close, and I feel complete,
In your love, our hearts meet.

Deep in Your Eyes

When I look into your eyes so deep,
I see a love that makes me weep.
A connection that no words can define,
Our hearts together, perfectly aligned.
In your arms, I find my place,
In your love, I feel your grace.

The Rhythm of Us

Our hearts beat in a quiet song,
A rhythm where we both belong.
Your kiss, so soft, ignites a fire,
A love that fills me with desire.
Every touch, a dance so true,
In every moment, I feel you.

A Promise in the Dark

In the dark, I feel your warmth,
A love so deep, it knows no harm.
Every kiss, a promise made,
In your touch, my fears start to fade.
You are my heart, my soul's delight,
In your love, everything feels right.

Wrapped in You

In your arms, I find my peace,
A love so deep, it will never cease.
Your touch is gentle, your kiss so sweet,
In your love, my heart skips a beat.
I lose myself in every moment we share,
Wrapped in you, without a care.

The Softest Kiss

The softest kiss, your lips on mine,
A love that feels so pure, divine.
With every touch, my heart takes flight,
In your love, everything feels right.
No words are needed, just you and me,
In your embrace, I am free.

Sweet Death

It's the tickle of the tongue;
It's a long deep sigh;
It's everything sliding into place
Because we've been lured beyond the gate.

Whimpering sounds of protest
Can't ever be heard over the sound
Of the cicada's cry,
Because life is so short
We've but a single mission
To mate and then to die.

There's hazy languor in your eyes
As our bodies fade into fusion;
We're entering into that secret place
Where grammar, syntax, and arithmetic
Have no meaning;
It's an indolent dogmatism;
It's the act of conception.

The tantalizing brush of your lips
Destroys the remnants of my army;
I'm a trillion cell massive apparatus—
But you've reduced me to a spook,
A demon that wants only you.

To move sensuously over your flesh
Is to lose even the ghost

Of an idea I once had of something gone;
I'm dying in your arms;
And it's a sweet, sweet death.

In Every Whisper

Every whisper, every sigh,
A love so deep, it reaches the sky.
Your fingers trace my skin so light,
With every touch, you hold me tight.
In every kiss, in every glance,
I feel the magic, I feel the chance.

Every Nights

Every night it's the same dark dream;
And it always ends with a scream;
You're following me;
You're haunting me;
You know I'm not what I seem.

It's a black hot drenching heat;
Late at night on an empty street;
You're chasing me;
You're right behind me;
And you smell so eternally sweet.

You don't come from the human swarm;
You're of a distinctly different darkened
form;
You're touching me;
You're tongue is breaking me;
You're smoothly warm.

Life is complex and monstrous;
Pleasure at times is cancerous;
Your hand slides up;
And you find my cup;
Life should be always so wondrous.

Your nails dig deep into my skin,
Even as my head begins to spin;
You're a burning flame;

But I'll not cast any blame;
For you've given me an evil grin.

We're on the brink of a cool spring;
It's time to make you my all new king;
Your tongue finds mine;
And I can taste your bloody wine;
Please make my body sing.

I give in to a long deep sigh;
Tell me we'll never say good-bye;
Now comes the bite,
and I won't fight;
Even if it's time to die.

A Love So True

Your love is a warmth I can’t explain,
It soothes my heart and heals my pain.
In every breath, in every touch,
I feel your love, so pure, so much.
With you, I feel I’ve found my place,
A love so true, a warm embrace.

Soul's Dance

Our souls dance in the quiet night,
In every glance, in every light.
Your hand in mine, your heart so near,
I lose myself when you are here.
With every kiss, with every sigh,
We reach for the stars, you and I.

The First Touch

Your eyes met mine, and time stood still,
A silent promise, a quiet thrill.
Your touch was soft, yet full of fire,
Igniting a spark, a growing desire.
In that moment, I felt it all,
The first meeting, our hearts' call.

The First Kiss

Our lips met gently, not too bold,
But in that kiss, a story untold.
A spark of passion, a quiet flame,
In that moment, we weren't the same.
The world around us faded away,
As we shared our hearts in that first sway.

The Dance of Us

I like my body when it is with your
body. It is so quite new a thing.
Muscles better and nerves more.
I like your body. i like what it does,
I like its hows. i like to feel the spine
of your body and its bones,and the trembling
-firm-smooth ness and which,

I will again and again and again kiss,

I like kissing this and that of you,
I like, slowly stroking the,shocking fuzz
of your electric furr, and what-is-it comes
over parting flesh….

And eyes big love-crumbs, and possibly

I like the thrill of under me you so quite new
!!

The Dance of Us

The first time we touched, it felt so right,
A quiet dance in the soft moonlight.
Your hand in mine, a spark so bright,
I knew then, you'd be my night.
No words needed, just eyes that knew,
That first meeting, just me and you.

Unspoken Connection

When you held me close, I felt no fear,
Just a warmth that brought you near.
The world disappeared, it was just us two,
In that first meeting, our souls grew.
No need for words, we both could see,
That we were meant to be, just you and me.

The Beginning of Us

Our first meeting was soft and sweet,
A feeling so pure, a love complete.
Every touch, every glance so new,
I felt you deep, and you felt me too.
In that moment, our hearts aligned,
A love so deep, forever to find.

The Scent of You

The scent of you lingers in the air,
A fragrance so sweet, so soft, so rare.
It wraps around me, soft and warm,
A love so deep, a calming storm.
In every breath, I feel you near,
The smell of love, so crystal clear.

Fragrance of Our Love

Your scent is like a summer breeze,
Carrying whispers of memories.
It's in the flowers, in the rain,
A soft perfume that soothes my pain.
With every kiss, your scent I find,
A love so deep, so intertwined.

You Are My World

You are my sun, you are my moon,
With you, my heart sings a tune.
Your love is soft like gentle rain,
Without you, only left is pain.
Your smile is light in my dark night,
Holding your hand feels so right.
I love you more than words can say,
Forever with you, I want to stay.

My Heart is Yours

Your name is written in my heart,
No one can take, no one can part.
Your eyes shine like morning sun,
With you, my life is never done.
Every breath I take is you,
Every dream I see is true.
Hold my hand, never go,
I love you more than you know.

Love Like River

Like a river flows to the sea,
My heart runs only to thee.
Your touch is warm like summer air,
Your love is soft, beyond compare.
Every heartbeat calls your name,
Without you, I'm never the same.
Hold me close, never leave,
My love for you, just believe.

My First and Last Love

From the day I saw your face,
My heart found its sweetest place.
Your voice is music, soft and kind,
Your love is magic, hard to find.
Every moment feels so new,
Because I have only you.
In your arms, I want to be,
You are my love, my destiny.

Forever You and Me

Love is strong, love is pure,
With you, my heart is sure.
Like the stars in endless sky,
With you, I want to fly.
You are my smile, you are my pain,
You are my sun, you are my rain.
Every life, every birth,
I choose you, my love, my earth.

Your Love is Home

In your arms, I find my home,
With you, I never feel alone.
Your eyes tell a thousand tales,
Like soft wind in gentle sails.
Every moment feels so true,
Because my world starts with you.
No matter where, no matter when,
I'll love you once, I'll love you again.

Unseen Love

I never saw love, but I feel,
Your touch makes my heart heal.
Your voice is music, soft and bright,
Your presence makes my world right.
Every tear, you take away,
With you, I see a golden day.
No words needed, just your touch,
I love you, oh so much.

The Love in Your Eyes

When I see love, I see your eyes,
Soft as clouds in golden skies.
Your laughter fills my empty days,
Your love is light in endless ways.
I was lost, now I am found,
With you, my feet don't touch the ground.
Hold me close, never let go,
My heart beats only for you, you know.

Only You

No one loves me like you do,
No one sees my heart so true.
You are the dream I always see,
You are the love inside of me.
Like the sun and moon above,
You complete me with your love.
With you, my soul will always stay,
Forever, till my last day.

Endless Love

Love is not just words we say,
It's the touch that takes pain away.
It's the hand that holds so tight,
The heart that shines like morning light.
With you, I walk through storm and rain,
With you, there's never-ending gain.
Love is not just you and me,
It's our souls, wild and free.

The Aroma of Us

The air is filled with you tonight,
Your fragrance soft, your touch so light.
Like jasmine blooming in the dark,
Your scent ignites a lasting spark.
In every moment, I breathe you in,
The smell of love, where we begin.

A Breath of Love

The smell of you is all I crave,
A scent so sweet, it makes me brave..
Your perfume lingers on my skin,
A love that starts where it begins.
With every breath, with every sigh,
I find you here, you never lie.

Love's Essence

In the air, I feel your trace,
The warmth of love, your sweet embrace.
The scent of love, a fragrant kiss,
A silent promise, endless bliss.
Every breath I take is you,
In your scent, our love is true.

Tears on My Pillow

Tears falling like heavy rain,
Heart breaking with silent pain.
You gone, me alone,
Love is lost, all is stone.

Why You Left?

You promised, you swore,
Now I am nothing anymore.
You leave me, like dry leaf fall,
Now my soul is empty hall.

Unfinished Story

We wrote love on life's page,
Now torn book, full of rage.
You move on, I stand still,
Heart is broken, lost my will.

Alone Road

You left, I stand in rain,
Walking alone, hiding pain.
My heart calling, you not hear,
Love is gone, only fear.

Why You Changed?

Yesterday we laughed, today I cry,
You tell lie, but don’t say why.
Love was true, or just game?
Now only left your name.

Only Memories

Your voice, your touch, your smell,
Now only in memory's shell.
You left me without goodbye,
I just ask, why, why, why?

False Love

You love me? Big, big lie,
Now my love only dry.
You move on, I still here,
Crying loud, but none hear.

Gone Forever

Your hands once held mine tight,
Now you gone, lost in night.
Heart still waits, but you no see,
Pain is deep, won't let me free.

Dreams Broken

We dreamt together, walked so far,
Now alone, under broken star.
You happy, I in pain,
Love is lost, left with rain.

Fake Promises

You said forever, forever died,
Now I cry, my soul denied.
Love was sweet, now it’s sore,
You not mine anymore.

Vanished Love

Where you go? Where I stay?
No words left for me to say.
Love gone, like wind blow,
Heart in pain, eyes full flow.

My Heart Still Waits

You moved on, so easy way,
But my heart still cries each day.
I wish love was strong like me,
But you left, now I let it be.

Only Silence Left

Laughter gone, love no more,
Your footstep left my door.
Now only silence stay with me,
Once we were, now just memory.

Lost in Time

We were two, but now just one,
Love like sun, now no sun.
Tears are sky, heart is sea,
Pain is deep, won't let me free.

Last Goodbye

You leave me, no reason why,
You no look back, just say bye.
Now I walk with empty chest,
Loving you was my best.

Shattered Soul

Heart once whole, now broken part,
Love was song, now silent heart.
I loved you, but you not care,
Now my soul only air.

Love is Over

Your love was home, now just dust,
I gave you all, gave my trust.
Now I walk this world alone,
Feeling heavy like big stone.

Fading Love

You were sun, I was sky,
Now clouds cover, all is dry.
No light left, only pain,
Heart is broken, love was vain.

Heart in Pieces

Your love was soft, now like knife,
Cut me deep, end my life.
Not in body, but in soul,
Now just dark, no more goal.

Left Alone

We were one, now we two,
You found new, I still blue.
Once your world, now I'm none,
Love is gone, my heart done.

Forgotten Love

Your touch, your voice, your care,
Now all lost in empty air.
You moved on, left me behind,
Love was blind, now pain find.

Heart's Cry

My heart is shouting, you don't hear,
You moved away, no tear, no fear.
Was it love or just a game?
Now only left is your name.

No More Us

Once my moon, now no light,
Only darkness fills my night.
Your love faded, like sunset,
Now only left is regret.

End of Love

Your smile was my sunshine bright,
Now just shadow in the night.
Once we laughed, now I cry,
Love is gone, time to die.

Walking Away

I see you go, I want to call,
But you don't care, not at all.
You left me like old song,
Now I cry, all night long.

Painful Love

Love was sweet, love was high,
Now only pain, and goodbye.
You moved on, I am here,
Dying slow, my biggest fear.

No More Dreams

Once we dreamt, hand in hand,
Now I stand, sinking sand.
You gone far, love is dead,
Only sorrow left instead.

Cold Goodbye

Your voice now cold like ice,
Once was sugar, now no spice.
Love is over, no more we,
Now just empty inside me.

My Heart is Dead

Once I smiled, once I danced,
Now only pain, lost my chance.
Your love died, so did mine,
No more sun, no more shine.

Never Coming Back

You left me, walked away,
Not one word you chose to say.
Love is gone, I don't know why,
All I do is sit and cry.

Only Your Shadow

I look around, I see you not,
Once you cared, now you forgot.
Your love like wind, now just air,
I still miss you, but you not care.

Left Me Without a Word

No goodbye, no last call,
You just left, that's all.
I cry, I wait, I stay,
But you never look my way.

Rain of Tears

Sky is crying, so am I,
Your love left, I don't know why.
Rain is wet, so is my face,
Without you, life has no place.

Time Changed You

Same face, same voice,
But no love, no choice.
You changed, I remain,
Now only left is pain.

Heart Without Home

Your love was home, now it's lost,
Heart is broken, heavy cost.
You found new, I am here,
Drowning slow, lost in tear.

I Let You Go

I hold your hand, you pull away,
I beg, I cry, but you not stay.
I let you go, though heart say no,
Now love is gone, only pain flow.

False Hope

I thought you mine, you proved wrong,
Now my nights feel so long.
You smiled, but heart was fake,
Now my soul about to break.

One-Sided Love

I gave my heart, you played a game,
For you love was just a name.
I was serious, you were not,
Now only pain is all I got.

You Are My Life

You are my heart, you are my soul,
With you, my life feels full and whole.
Your love is soft like morning light,
Holding your hand feels so right.
When you smile, my world is bright,
You are my peace, my shining light.
Through every storm, through every rain,
With you, I forget all my pain.
Husband and wife, forever true,
My life starts and ends with you.

Forever Together

From the day we became one,
My heart beats for you alone.
Your voice is music, sweet and kind,
Your love is peace in my mind.
Every tear, you wipe away,
With you, I see a golden day.
Through every joy, through every fight,
You are my sun, my morning light.
Hand in hand, side by side,
Forever with you, my heart's pride.

My Strength, My Love

You are my strength, my power, my guide,
With you, I walk with love and pride.
When days are dark, you hold me tight,
With you, my world is always bright.
Your love is deep like endless sea,
In your arms, I'm safe and free.
Through every smile, through every tear,
You are my love, my heart so near.
No matter what, no matter where,
Forever, my love, I will care.

You Are My Home

Not just a house, you are my home,
With you, I'm never alone.
Your touch is warm like summer air,
Your love is deep, beyond compare.
Every moment, I feel so true,
Because my world begins with you.
Through every smile, through every pain,
With you, my love, I will remain.
My heart is yours, my soul is too,
Husband and wife, forever true.

Our Love is Strong

Our love is strong like mountain high,
With you, I smile, I laugh, I fly.
Your hands in mine, I feel so free,
You are the love inside of me.
Through ups and downs, through thick and thin,
With you, I know we always win.
No distance far, no time too long,
Our hearts will sing the same sweet song.
No matter where, no matter when,
I love you now and always then.

Heart to Heart

Husband and wife, heart to heart,
From the start, never apart.
Your love is soft, your love is kind,
You are always in my mind.
Your voice is peace, your touch is sweet,
With you, my world feels complete.
No storm can break, no time can change,
Our love is pure, never strange.
Hand in hand, through every fight,
You are my love, my soul's light.

My Love, My Life

Every morning, I wake to you,
With love so fresh, so deep, so true.
Your smile is sun, your touch is light,
You hold me close, you hold me tight.
No words can say what I feel,
But your love makes my wounds heal.
Through every laugh, through every tear,
You are my love, my heart so dear.
Husband and wife, soul to soul,
With you, my love, I feel whole.

Always with You

With you, my heart is light and free,
You are my world, my destiny.
Your love is warm like morning sun,
With you, my life is never done.
Every heartbeat sings your name,
Without you, I'm never the same.
Through every joy, through every pain,
With you, my love, I will remain.
Hand in hand, side by side,
With you forever, my heart's pride.

You Are My Heartbeat

You are my heartbeat, soft and slow,
With you, my love will always grow.
Your touch is peace, your words are kind,
You are always in my mind.
Through every storm, through every night,
You are my star, my shining light.
No matter what, no matter how,
I love you then, I love you now.
Husband and wife, forever true,
My life starts and ends with you.

Goodbye Forever

You loved me once, but not today,
You walked away, no words to say.
Now our story, torn in two,
I loved you, but who were you?

Last Tear for You

This is last tear, last pain,
No more crying in the rain.
You gone, I learn to smile,
Goodbye forever, after a while.

Together Forever

You and me, together we stand,
Holding tight, hand in hand.
Through every tear, through every fight,
You are my moon, my shining light.
No matter what, no matter when,
I'll love you now and love you then.
Through ups and downs, through thick and thin,
With you, I know we always win.
Forever together, love so true,
My heart, my soul, belongs to you.

Kiss me in the Morning

Kiss me in the morning when the sun shines through the shades
Pull me tight against you putting off the start of day
Tell me that you love me, then please tell me again
Place those kisses on my forehead, on my nose and on my chin

I feel your heat arising as the sun rays warm this room
With eyes closed tight I feel your hands dispelling all the gloom
I curl up on my side with my knees drawn to my chest
Envisioning all those things I know that you do best

Please kiss me on this morning; let your lips awaken mine
We'll stay right here all day and just leave this world behind
I'll do all those little things you see within your dreams
Take my time, I'll take it slow and then to the extreme

Oh! Kiss me in the morning as I hunger just for you
Whisper all those things that let me know your heart is true
What was that? A shadow passing o'er the new day's sun
With opened eyes, I am alone…the fantasy was fun !!

My Heart Belongs to You

You're the beat in my heart,
That keeps me alive.
You're the dream in my mind,
That helps me survive.
You're the hope in my soul,
That never lets me fall.
You're the voice in my ears,
That answers every call.
You are not just my love,
You are my whole life.

Always With You

You're the strength in my soul,
That makes me stand tall.
You're the answer to my prayers,
That saves me from the fall.
You're the hand that holds me,
When I feel weak inside.
You're the love that surrounds me,
My heart's safest guide.
No matter where life takes us,
I'll always be with you.

You Are My Strength

You're the voice in my silence,
That speaks with love and care.
You're the breath in my chest,
That keeps me standing there.
You're the shoulder I lean on,
When I feel weak inside.
You're the one who stays,
Through every storm and tide.
With you, love is endless,
A bond that won't break.

You're My Wife, You're My Life

You're the light that fills my sky,
The reason my heart beats so high.

With every breath, with every sigh,
I find my home in your loving eye.

You're the morning that starts my day,
The soft sunshine that lights my way.

Your laughter is music, sweet and true,
Every joy begins with you.

Through every storm, through every rain,
You held my hand, you took my pain.

When the world was dark and cold,
You were my warmth, my hand to hold.

You're the strength when I feel weak,
The gentle words my heart does seek.

You wipe my tears, calm my fear,
With you beside, I have no fear.

Every dream, you made it real,
With love so pure, with love to heal.

Through every fight, through every test,
You always gave me your very best.

You're my wife, my greatest prize,
The love that shines in both my eyes.

No matter where, no matter when,
I'd choose you once and once again.

Forever and always, through joy and strife,
You're not just my wife, you're my whole
life.

I was searching

I think I was searching for treasures or
stones
in the clearest of pools
when your face..,

when your face,
like the moon in a well
where I might wish…
might well wish
for the iced fire of your kiss;
only on water my lips, where your face…

where your face was reflected, lovely,
not really there when I turned
to look behind at the emptying air…
the emptying air.

I love your Lips

I love your lips when they're wet with wine
And red with a wild desire;
I love your eyes when the love light lies
Lit with a passionate fire.
I love your arms when the warm white flesh
Touches mine in a fond embrace;
I love your hair when the strands enmesh
Your kisses against my face.

Not for me the cold, calm kiss
Of a virgin's bloodless love;
Not for me the saint's white bliss,
Nor the heart of a spotless dove.
But give me the love that so freely gives
And laughs at the whole world's blame,
With your body so young and warm in my
arms,
It sets my poor heart aflame.

So kiss me sweet with your warm wet
mouth,
Still fragrant with ruby wine,
And say with a fervor born of the South
That your body and soul are mine.
Clasp me close in your warm young arms,
While the pale stars shine above,
And we'll live our whole young lives away
In the joys of a living love.

I do not love you

I do not love you except because I love you;
I go from loving to not loving you,
From waiting to not waiting for you
My heart moves from cold to fire.

I love you only because it's you the one I
love;
I hate you deeply, and hating you
Bend to you, and the measure of my
changing love for you
Is that I do not see you but love you blindly.

Maybe January light will consume
My heart with its cruel
Ray, stealing my key to true calm.

In this part of the story I am the one who
Dies, the only one, and I will die of love
because I love you,
Because I love you, Love, in fire and blood.

If ever we shall perish

If ever we shall perish

and become but specks

of dust, I hope the wind

carries us away to that

place you've always loved.

She had the most beautiful thing that I had ever seen

She had the most beautiful thing that I had ever seen

And it took only her laugh to realize

that beauty was the least of her.

Coffee is

coffee is

all well

and good

but i would

rather

have your

lips

kiss me

awake

every morning

I would love to say

I would love to say

that you

make me

weak in the knees,

but

to be quite upfront,

and completely

truthful,

you

make my body forget

it has knees

at all.

I'm jealous of the morning sun

I'm jealous of the morning sun

That gets to be the first to see you

Or the coffee cup

Who gets to kiss your sleepy lips awake

Let love

let love

kiss your palm.

tuck it into

your back pocket

or some other

safe place.

let it stay.

I will follow you

I will follow you,

my love,

to the edge of all our days,

to our very last

tomorrows.

You are the poem

You

are the poem

I never knew

how to write

and this life

is the story

I have always

wanted

to tell.

I Never Knew

I never knew about happiness;
I didn't think dreams came true;
I couldn't really believe in love,
Until I finally met you.

Every Thought of You

Each thought of you fills me with sweet
emotion;
I give to you my deepest devotion.
My fondest wishes you completely fulfil,
I love you totally, and I always will.

You're Perfect

Your femininity/masculinity attracts me;
Your steady strength supports me;
Your tenderness sustains me;
You're the perfect love for me.

I Don't Know English..

I see you smile, my heart beats fast,
I wish to tell you, but words don't last.
In my heart, love shines so true,
But in your language, I have no clue.

I try to speak, but my words fall weak,
My love is strong, yet I cannot speak.
Every "hello" feels small and shy,
How do I tell you? How do I try?

I know no poems, no fancy lines,
No perfect words, no magic signs.
But when I see you, my world feels new,
My heart just whispers, **"I love you."**

If love needs words, I might stay lost,
But my feelings are real, no matter the cost.
Look in my eyes, hear my heart's sound,
In silent beats, my love is found.

I don't need English, I don't need art,
I just need you to feel my heart.
So if my words ever come out wrong,
Just know I've loved you all along.

I don't know English

I

don't

know English,

I can't explain,
But my heart calls

Your name again and again.

Can We Be United Again?

Can we be united again, my love?
Can we bring back the stars above?
The days feel empty, the nights so long,
Without your love, nothing feels strong.

Can we forget all the wrongs, Femi, and talk?
Hold my hand, take that walk?
No more tears, no more pain,
Just you and me, together again.

Can we start our love once more?
Like waves returning to the shore?
Hearts once lost, now find their way,
Let's not let love fade away.

I miss your voice, your gentle touch,
I never knew I'd love this much.
No past regrets, no words unkind,
Just love that's pure, two hearts aligned.

If love is true, it never ends,
It bends, it breaks, but then it mends.
So tell me now, take my hand,
Can we begin again, just as planned?

Can You Forgive Me?

Can you forgive me for the tears I made?
For the hurtful words, the love that strayed?
I never meant to break your heart,
But now I'm lost, torn apart.

Can you forgive me for walking away,
Leaving your heart in shades of gray?
I was blind, I couldn't see,
That you were the best part of me.

The nights are cold, the days feel long,
Without your love, I don't feel strong.
I hear your voice in every song,
Wishing I could right my wrong.

Can you forgive the past we had?
Erase the moments that made you sad?
I promise to hold your heart with care,
To love you truly, to always be there.

No more ego, no foolish pride,
I just want you by my side.
Let's rewrite our story, start anew,
With love that's deep, strong, and true.

So tell me now, look in my eyes,
Can we let go of all goodbyes?
If love is real, if love is free,
Can you find it in your heart to forgive me?

Let's Begin Again

Let’s forget the past, let it fade away,
Like night surrenders to golden day.
No more sorrow, no more pain,
Let’s hold each other and love again.

The tears we shed, the words we regret,
Let’s leave them behind, let’s not forget—
Not to hold on, not to break,
But to learn, to heal, for love’s own sake.

Take my hand, feel my embrace,
Let’s write new memories in love’s own
space.
A fresh new start, just me and you,
A love reborn, pure and true.

Will you marry me?

I have no riches,

No golden rings,
But I promise love in the little things.

Through every smile,

Through every tear,
I'll stand beside you,

Year by year.
With all my heart,

So true and free,
I ask you now

__Will you marry me?

Not just today, but all my life,
I want you as my love, my wife.
Through every storm, through every sea,
Will you walk this road with me?
With all my heart, on bended knee,
I ask you now—Will you marry me?

I may not have the perfect way,
But my heart knows just what to say.
With love so deep, as wide as the sea,
I ask you now—Will you marry me?

My heart speaks

Your name every night,

But,

You see me

As

Just a passing light,
Loving you feels

Like losing a fight.

I

love

you,

but

you'll

never

know,

I hide

my tears,

I let

them flow,
Smiling outside,

breaking below.

I hold my love like a secret fire,
Burning alone with silent desire,
Yet, you walk away, never inspire.

I apologize for the wrongs I’ve done,
Whether I knew or hurt someone.
With a sincere heart, I ask today,
Please forgive me, in any way.

If my words have ever made you sad,
Or my actions turned moments bad,
Know that I never meant to be,
The cause of any misery.

Sometimes we hurt, we fail to see,
The pain we cause so carelessly.
Knowingly or not, if I went wrong,
I'm sorry now, I've known it long.

I seek no excuse,

I place no blame,
For any hurt,

I take the shame.
Knowingly or not,

If I made you blue,
From my heart,

I apologize to you.

We meet again where it all began,
Hearts still race, like they once ran.
The same old place, the same sweet view,
But this time, love feels deeper, true.

Once again,

We stand so near,
The place we met,

Still holds us dear.
Time has passed,

But love remains,
A spark reborn,

Through joy and pain.

The breeze still sings our old love song,
In this place where we belong.
Once strangers, now hearts entwine,
Meeting again, like fate's design.

Same place,

Same stars above,

But

Now we meet,

Wrapped in love.
A second chance,

Alove so true,
Destiny brought me back to you.

We meet again, just like before,
But this time, I love you more.
The past, the pain, all fades away,
As our hearts find home today.

Do you remember our first meeting in this café?
Eyes full of wonder, hearts lost in play.
The coffee was warm, but your touch was fire,
That moment still sets my soul on desire.

Do you remember our first meeting in this café?

Soft music played, love found its way.
Your laughter danced like a sweet old tune,
My heart was yours that afternoon.

Raindrops kissed the window that day.
Your eyes held stories I longed to know,
In that moment, love began to grow.

The way your laughter lit up my day.
From that moment, my heart just knew,
I'd spend my life loving you.

Time moved slow, yet slipped away.
From that day on, through thick and thin,
My love for you will never end.

Do you remember our first meeting in this café?

Do you remember your kiss, gentle and
true?
The stars above shined just for you.
In that moment, time froze tight,
Love was born in moonlit night.

Do you remember your kiss

our love's first start?
The touch of your lips stole my heart.
Even today, when I close my eyes,
I feel that magic, I hear love's sighs.

A secret promise our souls would keep.
My heart still races, just like then,
Wishing to feel that kiss again.

First Fight..

I remember our first fight, the tears in your eyes,
The quiet between us, the soft, sad sighs.

I reached for you, refused to let go,
Because love means fighting, as we both know.

I remember our first fight,

The words left unsaid,
The storm in your eyes,

The thoughts in my head.
I begged you softly,

I held on tight,
Love always wins,

Even after the night.

I remember our first fight,

The space in between,
You turned away,

But love stayed unseen.
I kept on trying,

Whispering your name,
Because without you,

Nothing feels the same.

Do You Remember?

Do you remember our first dinner date?
The nervous smiles, the twist of fate.
You watched me laugh, you watched me glow,
As candlelight danced, soft and slow.

You made me eat food, spicy and bold,
My lips burned hot, my face turned cold.
I begged for mercy, a taste so sweet,
But you had a plan—oh, such a treat!

I asked for dessert, something divine,
You leaned in close, said, **"You'll be fine."**
And before I knew, in front of all,
You kissed me deep, made my heart fall.

Eyes widened, whispers filled the air,
But in that moment, I didn't care.
Your lips were sugar, soft and true,
A taste of love, just me and you.

Laughter echoed, hands entwined,
That daring kiss, forever mine.
Spicy or sweet, whatever may be,
Every flavor is love with you and me.

His Silent Gaze..

Whenever I would leave the house,
He would look at you, quiet as a mouse.
No words were spoken, yet so much was said,
A love so deep, where silence led.

His eyes would follow as you stood near,
Holding emotions, raw and clear.
A longing gaze, a silent plea,
As if afraid to set love free.

The world kept moving, the days went by,
But in his silence, love didn't die.
Each glance he stole, each breath he took,
Spoke louder than words, like an open book.

Did you ever feel his unspoken call?
The way his eyes would tell it all?
The ache, the wish, the dream untold,
A love too strong, yet left on hold.

Maybe one day, when time feels right,
He'll break the silence, end the fight.
For love unspoken still finds a way,
And quiet hearts have much to say.

When I Saw You Cry

I lay in white, so weak, so still,
Lost in pain, against my will.
Machines would beep, time moved slow,
But then I saw your teardrops flow.

You stood beside me, eyes so red,
A silent storm, nothing said.
Your trembling hands held onto mine,
As if afraid to lose our time.

I tried to speak, to ease your pain,
To tell you love would heal again.
But all I saw was your broken face,
A love so deep, so full of grace.

In that moment, I knew it true,
No fear remained, just me and you.
Your love, your tears, your silent plea,
Was all the strength I'd ever need.

So wipe your tears, don't break apart,
I live, I breathe within your heart.
And when I rise, when I am free,
I promise, love, it's you and me.

Take care

Take care of me more than yourself,
Hold me close like your heart's own wealth.
Stay with me through dark and light,
Talk to me, love, all through the night.

Whisper to me when the world is still,
Let love speak where words can’t fill.
No sleep tonight, just you and me,
Hearts wide open, wild and free.

Take care of me, don't let me fall,
Wrap me in love, give me your all.
Let's chase the moon, the stars so bright,
And lose ourselves in endless night.

Talk to me, don't let time run,
Let's make the night a rising sun.

Your voice, my love, is all I need,
A melody soft, a song to heed.

No need for sleep, just stay with me,
Let's drift like waves upon the sea.

With every word, my heart beats fast,
Hoping this moment forever will last.

Take care of me, don't let me break,
Be my moon when my heart aches.
Stay awake, hold my hand tight,
Let's turn this silence into night.

Forget the clock,

Let time stand still,
Love me now,

With all your will.
Talk to me,

Let's dream so deep,
A love so strong,

We never sleep.

Your voice is the cure,

My sweetest peace,
Every word makes pain decrease.

Stay with me,

Don’t say goodbye,
Let’s talk till stars fade from the sky.

Take care of me, like I’m your own,
In your love, I’ve found my home.

Let’s talk all night, just hearts in flight,
Dancing in whispers till morning light.

In your arms,

I found my home,
Even the stars feel less alone.

Your love is the air I breathe each day,
Without you, my world fades away.

Even in silence, I hear your name,
My heart still burns in love's own flame.

No distance,

No time can pull us apart,
You live in the deepest part of my heart.

If love is pain,

I'll bear it all,
Just to be yours,

To rise and fall.

You are my wish,

My every prayer,
In your eyes,

I lose all care.

Hold me tight,

Never let go,
Without your love,

I break and fall low.

My heart beats only for you,
Without your love,

what would I do?

Even in dreams,

I search for you,
Waking up feels empty and blue.

If love is madness, let me be insane,
For in your arms, I’ll live again.

You are the only forever my heart ever knew.

Loving you is like breathing—I can't stop,
even if I try.

In every heartbeat,

Your name still lives.

Even if the world fades,

My love for you never will.

You are

not just a part

of

my poem,

You

are

Heart of

My

Life.

My Love, My Heart, My Forever,

There is a distance between us, but it has never been enough to weaken the love I feel for you. No matter how many miles stretch between us, my heart finds its way to you, whispering your name with every beat. I close my eyes, and I can feel your presence—I can hear your laughter, I can sense your warmth, and I can imagine your arms wrapped around me, holding me close, even when you're far away.

Every day without you feels incomplete, as if a part of me is missing, waiting to be whole again. The nights are the hardest because I lie awake, staring at the sky, wondering if you're looking at the same stars, thinking of me the way I think of you. I wish I could reach out and touch you, feel your heartbeat against mine, and whisper all the words that get lost in the distance.

But despite this longing, despite this ache in my soul, I know one thing for certain—our love is stronger than any distance. No miles, no time, no space can change what we have. Every message, every call, every moment we share reminds me that love is not measured by how near we are but by how deeply we feel. And my love for you is infinite.

I dream of the day when I no longer have to miss you, when I can wake up next to you, hold your hand without the fear of letting go, and look into your eyes without a screen between us. Until then, I will love you from afar, cherish every word you say, and keep you safe in the deepest part of my heart.

No matter how many miles, no matter how much time passes—**you are mine, and I am yours. Always.**

Forever and always,

Mr. Owl

www.ingramcontent.com/pod-product-compliance
Lightning Source LLC
LaVergne TN
LVHW091257150826
845673LV00006B/1451

* 9 7 9 8 8 9 7 2 4 4 9 1 1 *